Tickey, The Lonely Tickbird,

And Other Stories

D1670942

Published by Covos Day Books, 2001
Oak Tree House, Tamarisk Avenue,
PO Box 6996, Weltevredenpark 1715, Roodepoort, Gauteng, Republic of South Africa

E-mail: covos@global.co.za
Website: www.mazoe.com

First edition 1991 by Quote Publishers (Pvt) Ltd, Harare, Zimbabwe

Design and origination by JANT Design, Centurion, Republic of South Africa

Printed by Creda Communications

ISBN 1-919-87419-4

Dedicated to Michelle and Matthew

Tickey, the lonely tickbird,

and other stories

Written & illustrated
by
Pamela Kelly

COVOS DAY
Johannesburg & London

Contents

Tickey,
the lonely
tickbird

"OH, I am *so* lonely," sighed Tickey, waggling his lame foot, "it would be nice to talk to somebody." But he was quite alone, standing on the riverbank in the moonlight.

Sometimes he looked up at the moon and sighed. Sometimes he listened to the river sounds, to the swishing of dark waters through the reeds below the bank. Now and again his tummy rumbled, reminding him that he was hungry as well as lonely.

Tickey belonged to the Egret family. His brothers and sisters followed behind the big game animals eating the grasshoppers and other small creatures, disturbed by the game passing through the long grass. They also acted as guards for their large friends, warning them of approaching danger by uttering loud cries and making a great fuss. Much of their time was spent riding on the back of a rhino or a buffalo, and the birds and animals were always the best of friends. Except in Tickey's case. No animal could be bothered to make friends with a lame egret. He could not fly well enough to ride on a buffalo's back. So Tickey lived quite alone.

Well, it happened this night, while he was gazing forlornly at the moonlit river, that he heard a fearful

WHEEEZZZING …
SNOOORRRTING …
CRASHING!

Page 1

Out into the moonlight lumbered a great black buffalo. It was old Boris. Tickey recognized him at once by his one broken horn and dreadfully scraggy coat. Boris was the oldest, crossest buffalo in the valley, and even the tickbirds were nervous of him. Not one dared to approach him or volunteer to tidy him up.

When Tickey saw who it was, he hopped out of the way and stood partly concealed amongst the reeds while old Boris came down to the river's edge to drink.

Now every creature in the bush knew that Boris was not only short-tempered but also short-sighted.

He could not see anything more than three metres away from him, and even then he could see only a vague blurred shape.

As Tickey watched the old buffalo he had an *idea*! What if Boris was lonely too? Perhaps that was why he was so cross. Plucking up courage, he addressed the great shape before him.

"Er… good evening, sir," he ventured timidly.

There was no answer.

"GOOD EVENING, I said, SIR!" he repeated in a louder voice. Then he remembered that Boris was also rather deaf, so he shouted his greeting even louder the third time.

Boris stopped drinking, and raised his head. He peered through the reeds in Tickey's direction.

"Uggghhhrrr," said Boris, and returned to his drinking.

Tickey took heart and tried once more.

"BEAUTIFUL EVENING, ISN'T IT?" he said loudly.

"LOVELY FOR DINING OUT, DON'T YOU AGREE?"

Boris was so unused to being addressed that he just scowled and said nothing. He could only just distinguish the faint outline of the little tickbird in the reeds.

"Perhaps you are going out to dinner tonight, sir?" continued Tickey, trying to keep up the conversation. "I would like to dine out tonight as well, but no such luck. I have nobody to keep me company. It is no good dining alone, is it—Sir?"

"Why not?" said Boris suddenly, and his voice was terribly gruff. "I do. You have to look after yourself, you know. Company indeed! You youngsters are all the same, want to be spoon-fed all the time."

He turned away and began enlarging a hole in the mud by the river's edge so that it would fill

slowly with water. He was looking forward to a peaceful wallow in the oozy wet mud. It had been such a hot day, and a good wallow would reduce his body temperature, to say nothing of getting rid of some of the nasty tsetse flies that bother him so.

Tickey was most surprised to hear such a long speech from Boris. At least the old buffalo had answered him. It was heartening.

"Please, Sir, I don't want to be spoon-fed. I am just not very quick to arrive at dinner on account of my leg, you see."

Boris stopped work on his puddle, which was coming along nicely. "What is wrong with your leg?"

"I got in the way of a hunter when I was a little fellow. I have been lame ever since and I can't move as fast as the others. I am always later for everything." There was a lump in Tickey's throat. He felt suddenly very miserable and dreadfully alone.

There was a moment's silence, and then Boris spoke, "Nonsense! I cannot see too well, nor hear too well, but I manage perfectly without help. You don't have to feel sorry for yourself, bird. Get on and do something, that's my advice to you," and he lay down in the wet mud and began to wallow.

Tickey did not dare say anything more after that. He just watched in silence.

Suddenly a blood-chilling sound broke the silence! A sort of low rumbling cough! It was not too far away either, just across the clearing from the nearest line of bush.

"Lion!" muttered Tickey under his breath and began to tremble. He looked around for a place to hide. Then he noticed that Boris was still quite unconcernedly wallowing. True, lions did not often attack buffaloes, but sometimes if the lion was very  hungry, and the buffalo was very old … Well, he had heard of cases. Boris was undoubtedly old. He was also rather deaf, nearly blind, and, at the moment, at a real disadvantage. He would be an easy prey, if surprised.

A shadow moved stealthily in the last line of thicket, and Tickey caught a glimpse of a tawny head. It was a lioness. She looked lean and hungry. That was bad. A hungry lioness was much worse than a lion. And there was old Boris, blissfully unaware of the danger. He would simply have to be warned.

"Sir!" shrilled Tickey, "SIR!" But Boris was enjoying his wallow and did not hear him. What is more his ears were clogged with wet mud.

"SIR! BORIS!" called Tickey, hopping right up to the old buffalo and screeching into his ear. "Look out—LION!"

Just at this moment the lioness came into the moonlight. She was flea-bitten, and battle-scarred, and her thin flanks indicated that she had not eaten for several nights. Her attention at once became riveted upon the buffalo, and she crouched low. Normally, she would not have attacked such a big

fellow as Boris but he was old—and he was lying on his side! She began to move forward stealthily, with her belly close to the ground and her eyes glittering.

Tickey was frantic with fear! He jumped onto the old buffalo's thick muddy neck and began hopping up and down, screaming into his mud-packed ear.

"LION! LION!"

This time Boris heard. At once he reacted to the warning. In spite of his age he was up on his feet with remarkable agility. Tickey did not have time to jump off so he clung precariously to Boris's neck.

The lioness began to cross the clearing. Boris grunted sharply and raised his head until his great horns lay along his back. His nostrils flared.

Then he caught sight of the lioness. With one movement he lowered his head to one side and swung it around to impale his enemy. A split second

before the lioness reached her prey she must have had second thoughts, for she swerved, hesitated, gave a short grunt of frustration, then headed back into the bush where she blended into the night shadows. All was silent once more.

"Okay," said Tickey in a shaken voice, but much relieved that the tense moment had passed without mishap. "She has gone, now." He looked about him, wondering how he could alight. His heart was still hammering within him and he did not feel very brave.

Boris suddenly began to paw the ground. He grunted several times. Then in his usual grumpy voice, but with quite a kind note in it this time, he addressed Tickey."You can stay on my back if you like. I think I need a bit of de-ticking. If you think you can manage the job …"

"I am sure I can," interrupted Tickey excitedly, "just give me a chance and you will see."

Well, from that time onwards, Tickey and old Boris became the best of friends. They were rarely seen apart, and the little bird took great care of his old friend, keeping him clean and tidy and keeping a sharp lookout on his behalf. In return for such care and devotion, Boris would get down on the ground and allow Tickey to hop onto his back, so the arrangement worked out very well in the end.

Needless to say, all the other tickbirds in the valley were absolutely amazed to see little lame Tickey in the company of Boris. They no longer dared to make fun of him, but treated him with the greatest respect. Of course, Tickey never told them the secret of how he had made friends with Boris. That would have meant letting Boris down, for then everybody would know just how blind and deaf the old buffalo had become, and that would never do.

So Tickey, the little lame tickbird, was never lonely or hungry again, but lived happily with his friend in the valley for many more years.

Annie
and the
iron trap

"SNUFFLE! Snuffle!" Annie Aardvark snuffled along in the undergrowth beside the farm road, looking for her supper. "There *must* be a termite nest somewhere near," she mumbled to herself.

Annie was plump and very shy. She always ate ants for dinner. With her tremendously strong claws she could dig a hole big enough to hide in within minutes, and Annie was as big as a mother pig! Nevertheless, she was much too shy to hunt in daylight. This particular night was ideal for hunting. The moon was on the wane and the bush had plenty of shadows, which gave her protection.

"Sniffle! Sniffle!" Her pig-like snout twitched anxiously. Now, if only she could find an anthill, she would make short work of it. With her long sticky worm-like tongue, which she could stretch to double its normal length, she would scoop up dozens of delicious ants. "Ummmh! Umh!" she grunted happily in anticipation of her favourite meal. She redoubled her efforts to find her dinner.

At this precise moment a farm truck came rumbling down the road. Blinded by the brilliant headlights Annie stumbled, but quickly picked herself up and scuttled off into the darkness as fast as she could.

In her anxiety to escape the cruel lights, she forgot her usual caution. For a moment her uncanny gift for sensing traps deserted her. There was a sharp 'SNAP!' Annie cried out in pain. But it was too late. Her paw was caught in the iron jaws of a trap. Frantically, she tugged and twisted, exerting all her strength. Then all at once she was free and rolling over backwards.

"I'm free! I'M FREE!" exulted Annie. Then the pain became so intense she could hardly bear it. She looked at her paw and found two of her powerful claws had been broken off in her struggle with the trap. In spite of the pain, she limped away into the shadows as fast as she could and finally stopped under a tree. There she stood on three legs, licking her paw and moaning softly to herself.

Now in the branches
of that tree sat Ortrud,
the barn owl. She was
just contemplating the
prospect of a little something for herself when
she heard Annie stumb-
ling through the under-
growth. Ortrud blinked
twice and stared down
at Annie.

"Whooo-Whooo!"
she exclaimed. "If it isn't old Annie Aardvark!" As
she peered through the branches she saw Annie
licking her paw.

"Whooo-what's up, Annie?" she called down from her perch.

"I was c-c-caught in a t-t-trap," sobbed Annie, "and I have lost two claws. I-i-it hurts terribly, you know," and her sobs became louder.

"Whooo-Whooo!" said Ortrud, shaking her head and blinking rapidly. "I'm surprised at *you* getting caught in a trap, Annie, really I am. I would have expected more caution from you."

"It was th-th-ose truck he-headlights b-b-blinding me," explained Annie, between sobs.

"Whooo-Whoo! I understand very well," Ortrud sympathized. "The wretched things ought to be banned—taken off the roads. They are a danger to all us night creatures."

Before she could say more the air was rent by high-pitched cries, rapidly growing louder as they approached the tree. In a matter of minutes the branches began to sway, and Ortrud was confronted by three pairs of saucer-eyes glittering in the darkness.

"Hello, Ortrud. Isn't it a lovely night for hunting up a good dinner?" There, before Ortrud, bounced Benji the bushbaby, accompanied by his wife, Berta, and little baby Bella, clinging to her mother's back.

Ortrud shut her eyes. They were such a noisy family but she could not very well be rude to them and they were always so cheerful.

"Whooo-Whoo!" said Orturd. "I was just about to go out to dine when I was interrupted by Annie."

"What's wrong with Annie?" asked Berta, bouncing baby Bella about on her back to keep her quiet.

Ortrud pointed to the dark moaning bundle on the ground. "She was caught in a trap and she has lost two claws and it hurts terribly," she explained to the bushbabies.

In no time at all Benji, Berta and baby Bella were all on the ground beside Annie, chattering sympathetically and shaking their heads.

"How are you going to find your dinner, Annie?" asked Benji in worried tones.

"She can't dig with her hurt paw—she will starve," cried Berta in distress.

Little Bella burst into tears. "P-poor Annie," she sobbed.

Ortrud blinked several times to keep back her tears. "This will never do," she thought. "As a member of the Wise Owl family, I must think of a way to help Annie." She shut her eyes in concentration. "Whoo-Toowhit!" she suddenly hooted, and without a word of explanation she vanished silently into the night.

Benji and Berta looked at one another, but neither could guess what had made Ortrud depart so abruptly. In the meantime, they felt they had to do something to help so they gathered leaves and, dipping them in a nearby spring, laid them gently on Annie's inflamed paw; but the pain was still very severe.

"Toowhit-Toowhooo!" exclaimed Ortrud triumphantly as she reappeared ten minutes later, to settle once more on the lowest branch of the tree. "He is coming! If anyone can help Annie, *he can*."

"Who?" asked Benji, Berta and baby Bella in concert.

"Doctor Py, of course," said Ortrud impatiently. "Doctor Pythagoras Python, to be more correct," she added in a superior tone. "He is a very good friend of mine and a first-rate M.D. (Herpt)."

The Bushbaby family was impressed and even Annie looked hopeful.

Soon Doctor Py arrived, carrying his doctor's bag containing a jar of ointment made from certain special herbs. He assured Annie that the ointment would heal her wound in a very short time. It was a special remedy, passed on from father to son in his family.

"Letmeseee," he said examining Annie's paw. "Ssssoooo, it-isss-painful-isss-it-not?" He opened the jar without further enquiries and began applying the ointment to the inflamed paw.

"You-must-not-worry, Annie," he soothed. "Thisss-will-sssoon-sssend-down-the-ssswelling-and-those -clawsss-will-grow-again, you-will-sssee."

Everybody watched with admiration as he quickly bandaged the paw, and started to pack away his doctor's bag.

"Lotsss-of-ressst-and-sssleep," he advised, smiling kindly at Annie. "I-count-on-your-friendsss-to-sssee-you-have-plenty-of-sssleep."

"Oh, how can I ever thank you, Doctor Py?" said Annie. "My paw has already stopped throbbing. I am sure I will get well soon now."

"Thatsss-the-ssstuff, thatsss-the-ssstuff!" exlaimed Doctor Py. "Thisss-ointment-hasss-magical-propertiesss. You-will-sssoon-sssee."

Then he said goodbye to Annie's friends, and away he slithered to visit his next patient. "Goodbye, Doctor Py," they called after him. "Thank you very much for your help," but the good doctor was already hurrying through the undergrowth on his rounds.

Then the friends helped Annie into a deserted aardvark hole where she could rest in safety.

"What a night!" exclaimed Benji, and his family agreed.

"Whoo! I'm off to dinner," announced Ortrud. "A nice plump mouse would go down well after all the excitement," and away she flew like a ghost in the night.

"So are we," chorused the Bushbaby family, and they too departed, leaping from branch to branch in search of fruit or insects and moths. As their chattering cries died away into the night, Annie fell fast asleep in her warm dark tunnel.

It only remains to say that Annie's claw *did* grow again, and she was soon able to dig out ants as well as before. As a token of gratitude she invited Doctor Py, Ortrud and the Bushbaby family to a moonlight picnic.

For the occasion Annie excelled herself with the food she provided for her friends. There were frogs served with a French sauce for Doctor Py, baked mouse for Ortrud garnished with marula fruit, and for Benji and his family a delicious sweet made from the sugary juice of palm stems.

It was a very jolly affair, and everybody enjoyed themselves so much that the party broke up in the early hours of the morning and they all went home singing lustily. It was probably the effect of some of the palm juice, which had fermented slightly and made them all feel just a little tipsy!

Impy finds
the king

ISABEL was the most beautiful impala doe in the herd, and her son, Impy, was the naughtiest, bounciest, and most inquisitive of all the younger members. He hardly ever listened to his elders, never stood still for a minute, and was always going off exploring on his own.

"Now do keep still for just a minute, Impy," begged Isabel. "I want you to listen to me carefully."

"Yes, Mum," said Impy, bouncing like a yo-yo around his mother. "Wheee! Look how high I can jump, Mum—just look!" And up and down he went like a coiled spring, his little tail a-flip.

"*Impy!* Will you *please* stop leaping about. I want to talk to you."

Impy stopped bouncing and gazed wide-eyed at his mother.

"I want you to promise me that you will not wander away from the herd today. Your father has been talking of moving on to a new area where we will all find more to eat. He is our leader and we must obey him. Now, I cannot concentrate on what he has to tell us if a part of my mind is worrying about you. Do be a good boy, just this once, and play with your cousin, Ignoo, while I attend the meeting. Ignoo never wanders away from the herd. It will ease my mind to know you are with him. Promise you will keep out of mischief for just a little while?"

Impy pulled a face. He stuck his long tongue out in distaste, and did a hop-and-wriggle-and-twist, all in one. He did not like his cousin, Ignoo. He was such a goody-goody. He never did anything wrong.

"Tongues are used for browsing, Impy," said his mother reprovingly. "They are not to help you pull nasty faces, so just you tuck yours in again, if you please." Impy had been practising how far out he could stick his tongue and how far around it would go to each side. Now he knew his mother was getting really upset, so he stopped teasing her.

"Okay Mum. I'll be good. You go along to your meeting and I'll just look for Ignoo." Isabel smiled gratefully at her son and, giving him a quick lick on top of his head, away she bounded to join the rest of the senior members of the herd.

Impy went in search of Ignoo. He did not really want to play with his cousin but he had promised his mother he would. Ignoo would not be far away. *He* never strayed from the herd—that was because he was such a scary-goose.

Impy had only gone a little way when he suddenly had an *idea*! He and Ignoo would go in search of the *king*! He had never seen the king. Ignoo had never seen the king. What an adventure that would be! Nobody in the herd would tell him anything at all about His Majesty. In fact they simply refused to discuss the subject. There must be some mystery about him. Well, the only way to solve it was to visit the king himself.

Carried away by his wonderful idea, Impy leaped high into the air several times, bounded this way and then that way, and when he had finished he forgot which way he had been facing. In fact, he seemed to be in a patch of thicket he did not recognize. Of course, he would just have to walk methodically around it until he could see what was on the other side.

"Good heavens!" exclaimed Impy in astonishment. Two long tree trunks, crossed one before the

other, confronted him. They were a very odd shape, knobbly and quite splotchy further up. He could not remember seeing a tree quite like this before. Of course, he could not see the top from where he stood, so he just gathered himself together and sprang high into the air to have a look.

"Well! You never know what strange things you might see in the bush, do you?" he remarked to himself when he had reached the ground again. He had glimpsed an ENORMOUS pair of eyes, set in the ODDEST face, on top of the LONGEST neck he had ever seen! Really! What on earth could it be? He would just have to ask.

"Hi, up there!" he called. "What are you?"

A very large pair of eyes, fringed by extra long lashes, blinked down at him but there was no answer.

"Did you hear me?" shouted Impy, doing a series of impatient little hops-and-twists. "What is your name?"

The long neck curved gently down toward him and there he was, looking straight into the enormous eyes and then … Ugh! A long, narrow grey tongue came out and licked him.

"Stop that!" shouted Impy, when he could get his breath back. "I don't want to be licked—what are you anyway?"

The big eyes blinked rapidly, and then in a rather husky, grunty sort of voice the creature answered.

"My name is Mopey —I'm a giraffe." And so he was, a baby giraffe.

In spite of the difference in size, the two were soon the best of friends. Mopey was a sweet-tempered fellow, and he and Impy were getting along famously when the *idea* popped back into Impy's head.

"Mopey, have you ever seen the king?" he asked. The baby giraffe wrinkled his nose, blinked a few times, and then silently shook his head.

"Well, I've been thinking," said Impy, "what if we go and visit him? I would like to see him just once, wouldn't you, Mopey? Whenever I mention the king at home my family always change the subject. What do you suppose could be wrong with His Majesty?"

Mopey furrowed his brow and slowly shook his head. He did not know. His family, too, refused to mention the king. But a king was a king and worth a visit, decided Impy.

"Come on Mopey. Let us call on His Majesty."

The baby giraffe's brows furrowed more deeply. He looked quite unhappy. "Oh, come on," urged Impy, bouncing up and down with excitement. "You are as scary as Ignoo, only he is small, like me, and you are such a big chap. You should not be afraid of anything."

That did it. Mopey and Impy set off at once through the bush. Impy darted and leaped and ran all over the place, while Mopey loped along at a steady pace. Both his legs on one side would go forward together and then both legs on the other side would move forward together. He did have an odd gait.

The bush was very dry, as it was halfway through winter and it had not been a good rainy season. Now and again they would stop to browse. Mopey used his long, pointy tongue to strip the leaves off the topmost branches of the thorn trees. When they found a mopani tree with a few leaves still on, Impy would browse from the lower branches when he could reach them.

They had not been travelling long when who should they see in the branches of a thorn tree but Mrs Mamba, wearing a very large sunhat. With her were her two sons, Martin and Malley.

"Good morning, Mrs Mamba ... morning boys." Impy greeted them politely, and because it was such a lovely exciting morning, he added, "Isn't it a glorious sunny morning?"

"It'sss-too-sssunny-for-me," replied Mrs Mamba in a hissy sort of voice. "I-sssimply-hate-thisss-sssizzzling-sssun. I-don't-know-how-I-ssshhould-manage-without-my-sssunhat." With a wriggle and a jerk she resettled her wonderful hat more comfortably on her head. It had a large shady brim with bright flower trimmings, and it was tied under her chin with a bright pink ribbon!

Impy dared not smile at the good lady's strange appearance. He had heard that she had a quick temper and it would be very unwise to offend her.

"It is a very fine hat indeed, and such excellent protection against the sun," he commented tactfully, while Mopey seemed quite dazzled by the headgear. Of course, Mrs Mamba was now in an excellent mood.

"Where-are-you-two-young-onesss-going-alone-through-the-bussshh?" she asked kindly.

"We are going to look for the king," burst out Impy excitedly.

Mrs Mamba looked startled!

"Do-you-know-where-he-livesss?" she enquired.

Impy and Mopey looked confused. The fact was that they simply had not given the matter any thought.

"I-can-ssseee-you-need-help," announced the good lady. "I'll-come-and-ssshhow-you-the-way. Come-along-boysss-put-your-capsss-ssstraight-and -follow-me."

Without wasting any more time she slithered down from the tree, followed by Martin and Malley. The two young mambas kept jostling one another.

"SSSt! Martin-and-Mally-ssstraighten-your- capsss," she hissed, and they were wise enough to obey.

Soon the party was off through the bush, Impy bounding along in front followed by Mrs Mamba and her two sons slithering at astonishing speed over the ground, with Mopey and Impy bringing up the rear.

After they had been travelling for some time, Mrs Mamba called a halt. "Pssst! Sssoftly-now-not-a-sssound-not-a-whisper," and she began to slither silently across a clearing toward a big thicket. As they drew near they all heard the queerest sounds coming from it!

"Fffuuurrrgh … ffuuurrrgh … ffuuurrrgh …"

"W-w-hat's that?" whispered Impy, his skin beginning to prickle and his tail flipping from side to side with fear. Mopey's rubbery nose and lips twitched nervously. His long tongue flicked in and

out and his mouth felt dry. He rolled his eyes fearfully.

"Pssst! He-isss-in-there. He-isss-in-the-thicket. Sssstep-sssoftly," hissed Mrs Mamba, gliding forward soundlessly. Martin and Malley clung to one another and kept close to their mother. Impy and Mopey followed, step by step. Then Impy halted on the very edge of the thicket.

"You have the longest neck, Mopey. Stretch over the thicket and tell us what you see," he urged. Mopey was reluctant. Impy prodded his legs with his small sharp horns. "Go on, be brave." Much against his will, Mopey proceeded to crane his long neck over the thicket. Impy saw his eyes grow wider ... and WIDER ... and WIDER ... until they nearly popped out of his head! This was too much; he simply had to look for himself. Cautiously he moved up and peered through the long dry grass.

Goodness! So this was the *king*! Massive golden head upon his huge paws, he slept off the effects of an excellent meal. His great tawny body was quite relaxed, but the watchers noticed the rippling muscles in it. The snores were regular and very loud. For a while the friends remained spellbound.

"Buzz ... Bzzz ... Bzzz ..."

Without warning, a bee, on his way home from a foraging expedition appeared, hovering above the king's head. The watchers stared in horror as His Majesty's whiskers began to twitch, and then his

ears twitched, and his snore turned into a snore-sneeze-roar—and then his head moved!

With one accord the friends reversed. Silently and swiftly they crossed the clearing, gathering speed as they ran. Only when they had put several kilometres between themselves and the king, did they stop to get their breath back.

"Sssooo," said Mrs Mamba smiling knowingly, "are-you-sssatisfied?"

"Y-yes, thank you Mrs Mamba. It was very good of you to show us the way to the king, b-but I do hope you will not mention this adventure to our parents, please."

"Of-courssse-not," replied Mrs Mamba, "but-be-wissse-and-ssstay-home," she advised.

"We will, don't worry," said Impy, as she and the boys climbed into a convenient thorn tree, "and thank you for your help, Mrs Mamba."

Then off the two friends raced to their anxious parents.

"Let sleeping kings lie, don't you think, Mopey?" said Impy after a while. "But all the same, I think it was a grand adventure, don't you?"

Mopey nodded vigorously, but he was just very happy to know it was all over at last.

When Impy reached home he found poor Isabel frantic with worry.

"Where have you been, you naughty boy?" she exclaimed anxiously.

"Oh, I have found a new friend, Mother," he said quickly, "his name is Mopey and he is a baby giraffe."

Isabel sighed. "Well, baby giraffes make good friends, and *they* don't get into trouble like some baby impalas I know," and she looked meaningfully at her son. Impy's face was innocent.

"Mopey is such a quiet fellow, but he is a good friend all the same. I would like to play with him again sometime."

"I do not think you will be able to do that, Impy, at least not this winter, because we are leaving right away. Your father has decided to lead us to a place where we will be sure to find plenty of lush green leaves to eat. But cheer up. Next spring we will return here, and you will be sure to meet Mopey again."

Theresa in trouble

"THERESA!" called Mother Tortoise, "time for your afternoon rest. Come along, now. It's too hot to play outside."

"*Don't* want to rest. Don't *want* to rest," muttered Theresa rebelliously. "I'll … I'll … *run away*! That is what I will do. There are reeds by the river where it is cool and shady, and I can play there instead of resting."

Without answering her mother, Theresa at once set off for the river. She walked as fast as her wrinkly little legs could carry her.

Theresa was a young African hinged tortoise. She had pretty yellow ochre bumps on her shell, which were outlined in dark brown. It was a very tiny shell because Theresa was only eight centimetres long. When she grew up she would still measure only twenty-one centimetres, but she was a brave little creature. She was also stubborn, and quite determined to find her way to the river.

How the sun beat fiercely down upon her as on and on she plodded. There was no shelter on the way through the dry bush and she soon began to tire.

Even so, she would not give in. On … and on … and on … she struggled.

"I will *not* go to rest," she kept muttering to herself long after the sound of her mother's voice had faded into the distance. "I will *not* go to rest …"

Theresa struggled on over stones and rubbly baked earth, for it was winter. No rain had fallen for months and all was dry and brown, except on the riverbank. Her little bow-legs moved more slowly as the sun shone more fiercely. She was hot and tired and drops of perspiration trickled down her wrinkled cheeks.

"Not much further to go," she told herself cheerfully, for by now she was more than halfway to the river. Then came the moment of victory.

"There! I've done it!" exclaimed Theresa as, an hour later, tired but triumphant, she crawled into a clump of tall green rushes growing beside the river.

"Ah!" she sighed blissfully. "What a beautiful, cool and shady forest!" You must understand that the reeds were just like a forest to the little tortoise.

After a short rest she began to feel hungry. She searched carefully amongst the reeds for a millipede or a dead frog. Perhaps she could find a nice juicy snail. Goodness knows there were plenty in the bush, for she remembered all the big empty shells she had seen earlier.

Now she could see nothing amongst the reeds, not even a succulent or some fungi, for even that would fill a gap in her empty little tummy. There was nothing for it, she would just have to explore a little further.

Off she went, slowly threading her way through the tall reeds, feeling about with her tiny horny beak for something to eat.

As she searched, she sang a little song which went like this:

Reedy forest tall and green
Perhaps a millipede you've seen
—a millipede you've seen?

The round and jointed juicy kind
You know the kind I hope to find
—the kind I hope to find.

Or a snail with humpy shell
That would do me just as well
—do me just as well.

Then again on frogs I've fed
Only the frog must be quite dead
—the frog must be quite dead!

So she shuffled along, sometimes singing and sometimes poking and prodding the earth. Now and again she would stop and exclaim: "How deliciously cool it is! Much better than resting under a bush—much better."

Then …

SLITHER …
  PLOP!
    SPL … ASH!

Into the river she went, head first!

Poor Theresa. Bravely she struck out and found herself swimming.

"All very … well, being … able to swim," gasped Theresa, "but which … way is the … bank? How can I … see where … I'm going?"

Gl-ug! Ga-loopsh! She had swallowed some water and nearly choked.

Theresa decided that talking while swimming was silly so, rather fearfully, she now paddled along in silence. Soon she grew weary, but still there was no sign of land.

It was just as well that Theresa did not see a long dark shape slide noiselessly into the water from a mud island in the middle of the river. Her heart would surely have failed her.

Crafty, the old crocodile, had excellent sight. He could tell a tasty morsel when he saw one, even at a great distance. There was not a ripple or a sound as he launched himself into the water and glided silently toward Theresa.

It was indeed fortunate for Theresa that Helga was, at that precise moment, taking her usual midday stroll along the riverbed. Helga was an elderly hippopotamus with a warm heart. All her children had grown up and left home, but she loved all small creatures. She was a very kind and loving old hippo.

During the heat of the day it was her habit to browse along the riverbed, eating the aquatic vegetation. It was the most sensible thing for a hippo to do, as she hated the midday heat. So,

looking up through the cool green water, she was amazed to see four tiny wrinkly legs kicking just above her.

"Well! I do believe it is Theresa Tortoise! Fancy the silly creature swimming on the surface in the blazing noonday heat! How foolish young folk are." Then after a moment she added: "I can see she will not be swimming much longer if I do not help her at once."

From the riverbed she had a good view of the long dark shape with a white belly, sharp claws and great powerful tail, gliding purposefully toward the little tortoise.

"This calls for action," said Helga to herself. With surprising grace and speed she rose through the water and surfaced directly under Theresa. The little tortoise suddenly found herself lifted up and out of the water and safely riding on Helga's broad back.

"Thank you, oh! Thank you, Aunt Helga," gasped Theresa gratefully. "I do not think I could have managed another stroke."

"I daresay you couldn't, young Theresa, but then you may not have needed to try. Just look who is coming toward us."

Sure enough, old Crafty cruised up alongside Helga and Theresa's heart nearly stopped beating!

"Good afternoon, Helga," said Crafty in a rasping voice. "Are you going into the ferry business?" and

Page 45

he grinned wickedly, staring all the while at Theresa.

"Not really," replied Helga pleasantly. "Theresa and I are just taking the air on the river. It is so hot ashore."

"So it is! So it is," exclaimed Crafty, "but surely it is a bit unusual for you to be taking the air in the noonday heat?"

"Well, a change is good for us all, and Theresa wanted to see the river so here we are, cruising along most pleasantly." Then, addressing Theresa she said, "Have you seen enough young lady? Shall we go ashore?"

"Oh, yes p-please, Aunty Helga," stuttered Theresa "I h-have s-seen enough, thank you."

"I'll say goodbye, then," sighed Crafty, trying to hide his disappointment. "I wish you both a safe

journey to the shore." He grinned, showing a frightening array of teeth, and then silently submerged.

"Humph! That put him in his place," said Helga with much satisfaction. "I hope you will listen to your mother in future, young Theresa. After all, I may not always be near enough to come to your rescue. You would be wise to rest in the afternoons and not try swimming in the river. Remember you are not a terrapin. As you have discovered, there are some unpleasant characters in this river with nasty habits."

"Oh, I promise I'll never run away again," exclaimed Theresa most earnestly. "Really, I won't, Aunt Helga," and she meant it.

Just then they both heard an anxious voice calling from the riverbank. "Theresa! Oh, Theresa, where are you?"

"Here I am, Mother," Theresa called back.

What a happy reunion! Theresa told her mother all that had happened, and Mother Tortoise, with tears in her eyes, thanked kindly old Helga for rescuing her truant daughter.

"Oh, you are welcome," replied Helga, a little embarrassed. "I-I like young folk, you see, even if they *are* always getting into scrapes."

"Will you visit us often when you come ashore?" asked Mother Tortoise. "Perhaps you could have supper with us tomorrow evening? I know where there is an excellent patch of deliciously juicy grass which I feel sure you would enjoy."

"Why, that would be lovely," and Helga beamed at Mother Tortoise. "I do get lonely now that the children are gone, and it will be fun to dine in company."

"That is settled, then. We will call for you here tomorrow evening," said Mother Tortoise. "Until then, goodbye Helga, and thank you."

"Goodbye Aunt Helga," called Theresa, "and thank you for saving me from Crafty Crocodile."

With many a wave, Mother Tortoise and her daughter began their journey home, while Helga slowly walked back to the water's edge, glad to return to her browsing in the cool depths of the river.

Velia's midnight adventure

"MUM, I can't sleep," complained Velia.

"Nonsense!" said Mother Vervet crossly. "Do keep quiet, Velia. Others want to sleep, you know."

Velia twisted her mouth, but said nothing. Mothers could be very unfeeling sometimes and she might get a sharp smack if she continued to complain. Her little black face looked dejected and

she twitched her white eyebrows, scratched her speckled grey back, and examined her black-tipped tail minutely for fleas. Not that she could see much, but it passed the time.

It was late evening. The Vervet troop, all twenty of them, had just settled down for the night. Except Velia. There was a half-moon, and it often hid behind a cloud. When this happened it would become really dark, but just as suddenly it would pop out unexpectedly and throw a soft silver light over the bush. Velia felt wakeful and restless.

She was just closing her eyes during a nice dark patch when she heard scuffling in the undergrowth

below her tree. She peered down through the darkness.

At that moment the moon came out from behind a cloud and she could just see the shapes of the Warthog family.

Mr Warthog was a fearsome-looking fellow, with huge warts hanging under his eyes and stiff white bristles sticking out of his cheeks. He had wickedly curved tusks, and black bristles stood out along his neck and shoulders. He was very strong, and even leopards thought twice before attacking him.

Usually, he took the family out foraging for roots only on really dark nights. Well, it was quite dark when the moon was hidden behind a cloud, but moonlight could be dangerous to them all if they were careless.

"He must know what he is doing," thought Velia, "and Washington is probably around somewhere."

Washington was most certainly there, right below Velia's tree, and Washington was her special friend.

"Psst!" she called down to him. Washington stopped grubbing and glanced up at Velia.

"Oh, it's you!" he said ungraciously, and returned to his search for food.

In seconds Velia climbed silently down to the ground. She spoke in a whisper. "I can't sleep, Washington."

Washington just grunted. He did not have very nice manners, and he was interested only in his dinner anyway. Velia had an idea! "Do you think I could come foraging with you and your family? I do love those juicy roots your mum and dad always dig up, and I am beginning to feel peckish."

"Of course you can't come by yourself stupid," snapped Washington, "your folks would not like it—neither would mine," he added.

"Oh, my folks are asleep. They won't even know," begged Velia. "I will be good, I promise."

Washington was doubtful. Velia looked so appealingly at him that he finally weakened.

"You had better move smartly. My folks have gone on ahead now, you and your chattering," and he trotted vaguely in the direction he thought his parents must have taken.

They threaded their way through the bush, Washington in the lead trotting purposefully with his spindly black-tufted tail held stiffly erect, and loping along just behind him came Velia.

"Isn't this exciting?" she exclaimed in a loud whisper. "I do love foraging at night. You must have such fun, Washington."

But Washington did not answer. He was feeling just a little nervous, as he could not pick up the trail of his parents and he was not used to wandering through the bush on his own yet.

"Just stop chattering, will you, Velia? No sense in attracting unwelcome attention you know."

A very wise observation, but it came too late! At that very moment they were crossing a small clearing when the moon suddenly came out and …

THERE …
   SHE …
      WAS!

Lucia Leopard, reclining gracefully along a low branch, was staring with her yellow-green eyes straight at the two young foragers!

Washington and Velia froze in their tracks!

Lucia looked faintly surprised! She found it hard to believe her good fortune!

"Two dear delectable little morsels trotting through the bush all by themselves. Not a parent in sight! Well, well," she purred softly. "It is my lucky night. I could just do with a snack." She began to flex her muscles in preparation for a spring, but she was in no hurry. This snack was practically in the bag.

All the time Washington and Velia had remained rooted to the ground in fear. Suddenly the moon vanished behind a cloud.

"Quick, Velia follow me," snapped Washington and shot off at an angle into a thicket.

Velia leaped after him. Both were aware of the powerful speckled enemy somewhere in the darkness, not too far behind. It would not be long before Lucia caught up with them.

Then, in a flash, Velia suddenly left the trail along which her friend was racing, and in one movement leaped into a tree. She began screaming and chattering at the top of her voice.

Lucia was thrown off guard for a moment, and Washington was able to put a greater distance between them. Velia kept jumping up and down and shrieking her warning to all the creatures in the bush.

Lucia hesitated. She had half a mind to climb the tree after the silly vervet but decided against it. She coughed angrily, then dashed off in pursuit of Washington.

Of course, the noise Velia made alerted her troop. They all arrived in minutes and joined the chase. The noise was deafening. They followed Lucia through the bush, leaping from tree to tree, screaming their warning that Lucia Leopard was on the hunt.

Mr and Mrs Warthog heard it just as Washington came racing headlong through the bush.

"Into that aardvark hole, quick," said Father Warthog. Washington and his mother slipped in, while father turned smartly at the entrance, his rear end in the burrow and his great tusks facing Lucia. From this vantage point he resolutely faced the leopard.

Lucia looked disgusted. She knew she could do nothing now. With all the screaming from the Vervet troop the whole bush must have been alerted, and everyone knew she was after something. As for Father Warthog, she certainly did not intend engaging him in battle. He was a formidable opponent, especially in his present position. Oh well, perhaps it was not her lucky night after all. She turned and silently melted away into the darkness.

Of course, the whole troop of vervets lectured Velia, but they did agree that she had proved herself to be both quick-thinking and brave.

Even Father Warthog grunted his thanks. Velia had certainly helped to save her friend, Washington, from a nasty accident that night.

"All the same," said Velia's mother severely, "don't you ever again get down from a tree alone at night, my girl, or I shall have to smack you soundly, do you hear?"

Velia heard, and she never did.

Horatio,
the film star

THE Ground Hornbill family was out for a walk in the forest. Father Hornbill had a very fine beak and looked extremely smart in glossy black and white. His scarlet throat provided a wonderful splash of colour. Mother Hornbill looked just as elegant. She was also most particular about the appearance of the children. They were considered the smartest and best behaved of all the young creatures in the bush. She often received compliments concerning her charming daughters.

"Why, Mrs Hornbill," Bertha Bushbuck would say, "what delightful children you have, always so neat and such lovely manners. I do congratulate you."

Mrs Hornbill would preen herself. "Hortense and Harriet, what do you say to Mrs Bushbuck?"

"Thank-you-ever-so-much-for-the-compliment," they would chorus dutifully, inclining their heads graciously as Mother had taught them to do. Then there would be a

RUSH ...
STUMBLE ...
CRASH!

Horatio would arrive in a cloud of dust! Always late, he would hurry along, trying to catch up with the party. Somehow, he always managed to trip over a tree stump or slide on some leaves, then turn head-over-heels and make a three-point landing, arriving on his tail feathers and heels, with his big feet in the air!

Poor Horatio. He was always tripping over things and being generally clumsy. This was not surprising really as he never looked where he was going. He found everything around him interesting, so that he would scurry along commenting on all he saw, but never looking at the ground before him.

Mr and Mrs Hornbill could hardly believe he was their son!

"Horatio!" Mr Hornbill would say sternly. "On your feet at once, do you hear? Jump to it, or else …"

"And kindly smooth your feathers at the same time," Mrs Hornbill would add coldly.

It was no use. He was always in trouble for disgraceful conduct and untidy appearance.

One day the family was going to visit their great-grandparents in another part of the country. The old couple were very strict about manners and neatness. After a serious discussion, Mr and Mrs Hornbill decided to leave Horatio at home. There was sure to be trouble if they took him along.

"I'm sorry, Horatio, but you will only upset your great-grandparents. You had better stay at home and try to keep out of trouble."

With that, his parents and his sisters all waddled down the forest path, all looking very smart indeed.

Horatio stood and watched until they were out of sight. He blinked back a tear. His beautiful long lashes were quite wet and shiny.

"Nobody wants me, nobody at all," he snuffled to himself.

But soon he consoled himself. "Well then, I'll go for a long walk on my own. Perhaps I will find an adventure."

He brightened at once, blinked the tears from his eyes and, without any further preparation, scuttled off in the opposite direction as fast as he could go, exclaiming and chattering to himself, falling over twigs, picking himself up and resuming his exploring without any thought of tidying his feathers.

He found some delicious new fruit and saw a number of creatures with whom he passed the time of day. None of them criticized his appearance. This pleased him very much.

Horatio had no idea how long he had been walking, but a moment came when he noticed the sun was setting and the shadows lengthening.

"Goodness! It must be quite late," said Horatio to himself, "and I had better be going back now."

But which way was back? He just could not remember. After a few attempts to find his way home he gave up. It was no use. He was quite lost.

"I will just have to carry on and ask the next creature I see how to get home."

So he continued on his way, asking as he went, but nobody could direct him homeward. Soon it was dark. He began to feel nervous. After all one could meet the wrong kind of forest dweller at night …

Just as he was considering getting up into a tree to roost for the night he saw a glow in the distance.

"What is that, I wonder?" Horatio's curiosity was at once aroused. As he waddled along through the darkening forest the light became brighter. Finally, to his astonishment, he found a camp with people sitting around a fire.

"How exciting! I wonder what they are all doing in the forest?" he asked himself, and as there was no answer, he there and then made up his mind to roost in a nearby tree until morning, when perhaps the mystery would resolve itself.

With first light Horatio awoke. He gave his strange booming call to greet the dawn. Then he watched the activity in the camp below. A lot of people seemed to be pulling monstrous machines with long cables, shouting to one another, and then

a lady emerged and began talking to a hunter. While they talked, the machines made the strangest whirring noises. Horatio found it all so fascinating that he was soon on the ground, drawing closer and closer to the camp. Then it happened! His claw became entangled in one of the cables; he tripped, and turned head over heels and landed on his tail feathers with his big feet in the air—right in front of the lady!

Well! There was an astonished silence. Then everyone began exclaiming, and the lady and the hunter stroked him. The lady gently picked him up in her arms and smoothed his feathers. The machines were whirring again and Horatio found himself being admired and petted by everyone, especially the lady. Somebody gave him some new delicious fruit, which he had not tasted before. It was lovely. Then more praise and admiration and stroking.

"This is the life," said Horatio to himself. "Everyone here likes me."

And so it was that Horatio joined the film unit, for the people in the camp were making a film. There were shots of Horatio in the lady's arms, being stroked; Horatio having dinner with the stars; even a shot of Horatio tripping over a cable, turning head over heels and making his famous three-point landing on his tail feathers! He was fussed over constantly, and everybody loved him. Horatio had become a star and he was blissfully happy. Of course, he now took great pride in grooming himself and his feathers became beautifully glossy.

Then one day it all came to an end.

The equipment was packed away, and the lady hugged him and wept a little. A beautiful broad gold band was placed around one of his legs. It was engraved with the words:

TO THE STAR OF THE SHOW
'HOLLYWOOD HORNBILL'
WITH LOVE FROM THE CAST AND CREW

"Well, well," exclaimed Horatio, admiring his bright and beautiful new ring. "Wait until the family see this!"

As the film unit moved off they waved to Horatio, calling: "Goodbye, Hollywood, goodbye." Horatio gave a special booming call, and then there was silence in the forest again.

When Horatio arrived home his family greeted him joyously. They were so pleased to have him back. And how impressed they were by this new elegant Horatio. They could hardly believe their eyes! "What is that on your leg, Horatio?" enquired his elegant sisters.

"That," replied Horatio, extending his claws so that his family could see for themselves, "is a present from the film unit with which I was working. You are addressing a famous film star, I'll have you understand. In future I would appreciate it if you would not call me Horatio but Hollywood—that is my stage name, you know."

Now that he was famous he no longer tripped over roots or slid on leaves. He became a bird of high standing amongst the hornbill community in the forest.

Indeed, Bertha Bushbuck would often say to Mrs Hornbill: "Why, you must be *so* proud of your famous son. You do have a way with children."

And Mrs Hornbill would smile, and incline her head graciously.